MODERN PROVERBS

To Bill and family,

Thanks for your friendship.
It's good to have friends that
share common interests.

Sincerely,

Mike Williams

MODERN PROVERBS

Michael G.
Williams

Printed and distributed
in the United States of America by

 Horizon
Publishers
& Distributors, Incorporated
P.O. Box 490 Bountiful, Utah 84011-0490

Table of Contents

Acknowledgments

I want to express my appreciation to
Darrell Redford, for the many hours
of assistance he contributed,
to my wife, Vicky,
and to my Heavenly Father, without
whose help and inspiration this book
would not have been possible.

Michael G. Williams

Attitude

With negative thoughts our attitude rots.

*   *   *

A chip on the shoulder is much uglier than any disfiguration.

*   *   *

Determination has no detours.

*   *   *

"I don't know" is a lot more intelligent than "I told you so."

*   *   *

Never let the sun set on your upset mood,
Or the night form scars of regret on your attitude.

*   *   *

We must keep a good lookout to have a good outlook.

Opinion

I believe people are entitled to their own point of view, and I respect their ideas and opinions, be they hobos or governors, but I wouldn't let either of them budget my finances.

*   *   *

A righteous opinion is often divided by unrighteous dominion.

*   *   *

Are opinions so offensive that our differences demand defenses?

*   *   *

I don't like people to ask me for my opinion when they really want me to tell them their opinion. They just want to hear their opinion from someone else.

*   *   *

Perception

Sometimes some things don't seem deep enough, or they seem too deep. Maybe it depends on our depth perception.

*   *   *

Shadow to one is shade to another.

*   *   *

The trick isn't turning the frog into a Prince, it's getting the Princess to kiss the frog.

*   *   *

We are either one of the crowd or one of the crowded.

*   *   *

Interpretation is not definition!

*   *   *

Maybe those who are slower to surface are diving for a deeper purpose.

*   *   *

There are more people afraid of depth than there are people afraid of height.

*   *   *

Curiosity saved the rat!

*   *   *

If the shoe fits . . . the right is always right until it is on the other foot. The shoe never fits right on the other foot.

Point Of View

Sometimes we think it's not in the cards, when we
ought to re-shuffle the deck.

*   *   *

It's good to have answers as long as we don't think
they are "the answers" to everything.

*   *   *

Whether you realize it or not, your point of view is
your point of you.

*   *   *

Division
When our vision is divided,
We'll always see two-sided.
I like to make one point
Concerning our point of view:
Some say it's not polite to point,
But I think it depends upon
What we are pointing to.

*   *   *

What we have in common is our point of view:
Yours points to me and mine points to you.

*   *   *

Character

A man is poor if he sells his character; no matter what the price!

      *   *   *

The stature of a man's character depends upon his outlook on people. No matter what the reason— prestige, wealth, prejudice, or simply self-righteousness; a man who looks down on others puts himself below everyone.

      *   *   *

A man who doesn't care how he acts has no character.

Courage

It takes courage to express yourself, but sometimes it takes much more courage not to.

      *   *   *

The difference between heroes and hermits is their ability to face reality.

Example

You can't apply your beliefs to someone else's life, but with love and example, you can help them apply their own.

*   *   *

How can someone tell you what you can't do who hasn't done it himself?

*   *   *

You can always tell what a man thinks of himself by the way he treats others.

*   *   *

Unfortunately, the greatest influence most people have on others is influenza.

*   *   *

You don't have to be a hit to make an impact.

*   *   *

Disrespect is one of the poorest examples of
    religion known;
If you don't respect what others believe,
You won't respect your own!

To Prophet, President, Poet, or Philosopher:
Whatever it was you stood for;
For all the truth through life you gave;
Your spirit and truth stand just as tall,
Though your body lies in a shallow grave.

* * *

For what kind of influence will you be responsible
One that's dominical or one that's demoniacal?

* * *

His life was a lesson profound,
For he was a charitable man.
In his actions and example
Sermons were found
That taught me more
Than any textbook can.

* * *

A free sample of example is much more valuable than
advice at any price.

Habit

We are always forming habits, even when we are
doing nothing. Unfortunately, the easiest habit to
form is the habit of doing nothing. The second easiest
is the habit of doing nothing about it. It is easier to
avoid a questionable action than to break a habit!

* * *

Time is the only difference between habit and instinct.

Maturity

Maturity is the age when your mother can no longer embarrass you.

* * *

We are starting to grow up when we feel the need to grow up, and when we stop complaining about what happened while we were growing up.

* * *

You can tell a person's level of maturity by his pacifiers.

Open-mindedness

It is just as wrong to not listen to another as it is to have the wrong answer to his question.

* * *

Everyone is open-minded and agreeable when it's to his own advantage.

* * *

Truth cannot survive in a closed mind. It suffocates.

* * *

Open-mindedness is the willingness to believe that you might be wrong so that you might learn to believe right.

*   *   *

What happens when a man with an open mind meets a man with a closed mind — will either of them change?

*   *   *

It's the borders and the boundaries of our mind that confine us.

Patience

The fastest way to find something is to avoid it.

*   *   *

The most dangerous thing about jumping the gun is that we usually jump in front of it.

*   *   *

Patience rewards in time payments,
Not in one lump sum;
How we invest our time determines
How our profits come.

*   *   *

My impatience has developed from aggravation I feel because of wasted time spent waiting for someone else.

Excellence

You don't have to stand out to be outstanding.

*   *   *

We can't achieve perfection in this life, but we can't achieve it in the next life either if we don't try in this life.

*   *   *

No one is outstanding who isn't also understanding.

*   *   *

Excellence always has an audience — an audience gifted with common sense, good intents and buried talents. Experience and expedience are the expense of excellence.

Accomplishment

Beginning gives us the power to finish. Whether or not we use that power depends on how much we want it.

The power of accomplishment fades away with every moment we delay.

*   *   *

We try to fail when we fail to try!

*   *   *

A man who doesn't know where he is going is just as unhappy as the man who is going where he doesn't want to go.

*   *   *

Decisions, like promises, have two parts:
1. Making them, and
2. Deciding which ones we are going to keep.

Ambition

In the constant battle between Satan and men
there is also a war that rages within;
Between the determination we have to win,
and the lack of determination to begin.

*   *   *

One becomes great by aiming for greatness, not by belittling everyone else.

*   *   *

Our limitations are because we recognize them as such.

What good is motivation without a motive?

*   *   *

A great ability for any man is the ability to commend instead of command.

*   *   *

To just be good enough is just not good enough!

*   *   *

We admire someone who is making a comeback as long as he doesn't pass us in the process.

*   *   *

Andy Warhol said that everyone would be famous for at least fifteen minutes, but he never mentioned how much time they'd waste trying to receive their fame, or how much time they'd waste in trying to retrieve it.

Competition

Any time we compete just to win we are losing.

*   *   *

May all that is competible also be compatible.

*   *   *

If everyone tried to pay attention as much as he tried to get attention, there would be more than enough for everyone.

* * *

The best of the worst is no better nor worse than the worst of the best. But then again, who wants to compete in that contest?

* * *

Why do we jest and why do we boast
About who's the best and who has the most;
After all, who's the guest and who's the host?

Dreams

When you wish upon a star,
You will not get very far.
You can never reach your goals
Chasing fantasies and rainbows.
If you would have your dreams come true,
You must plan and work to see them thru.

* * *

Life has two extremes;
We either focus on nightmares
Or we focus on dreams.

Endurance

The pressure of evil surrounds us constantly, like water around a submarine. If we open the door any at all, we can be flooded and destroyed. Just because we are submerged, doesn't mean we have to stay there. It we hold tight we'll come out on top.

* * *

Make sure you know what you can take before you take it.

* * *

The unavoidable is always inevitable!

* * *

No persistence, no resistance;
Life would be just existence.

* * *

Never coast! When the going gets easier we use our momentum the most!

* * *

No one is satisfied to merely survive unless he is suffering and struggling merely to do so.

* * *

What force or source gives us the power of persistence? Is it the resistance or our reactance that controls the conduct of our existence?

* * *

I used to say it was okay to stray
As long as we got back on the path again.
But I have since learned it is hard to return,
And we can never catch up to where we might
have been.

Success

Competition is wrong when someone benefits from another's failure. When someone fails we all fail, and when someone succeeds, we all succeed.

* * *

A man's a failure who succeeds alone.
Don't swim in suc-cesspools! Success has drowned a lot of failures.

* * *

Those who have tasted the sweet flavor of success can never quench the thirst, no matter how much they drink. Success is the icing on a cake with no filling.

* * *

Experience

Adam and Eve,
In their innocence,
Partook forbiddingly.
But only the most foolish
Would return again
To the tree.

*   *   *

Value and taste are both relative to experience. We cannot appreciate something until we learn to speak the language.

*   *   *

The wise man built his house upon the rock. I'll bet he built his house higher than the foolish man's house.

*   *   *

Great is the man who can live today and not live for the day; who can leave yesterday in the past and yet keep enough of it so that he will know better tomorrow.

When it becomes recognizable after it's irreconcilable, then we should learn to pay better attention!

*   *   *

There are two ways to solve problems: by using insight or by using hindsight. The key to finding a needle in a haystack is to use a very powerful magnet or a very sensitive behind.

*   *   *

I believe that this great truth applies to everything we experience: You can learn by it or burn by it!

*   *   *

Experience's lessons are always remembered longer than advice's.

*   *   *

Hindsight is the only way some people get enough insight to turn around.

*   *   *

Men taste the bitter that their thirst may be better.

*   *   *

Hindsight may be 20/20, but insight always is!

*   *   *

I'll never forget the things that he knew.
While he shared his experiences,
I got my share too.

*   *   *

Can you ever have too much experience?

Advice

Neither take advice from one who never takes advice
nor from one who always does.

*   *   *

"If I were you." What a stupid saying. How can
someone know what he would do if he were someone
else? He certainly hasn't experienced it. And besides
that, if I were you, who would you be?

*   *   *

You can say something that means something else,
and you can say something else that means nothing.

*   *   *

Taking advice is much like eating out. The menu is
full and there will be many to take your order. But
be careful, before you partake, to make sure none
of the ingredients in the recipe are harmful to your
health.

*   *   *

It's a sad truth that those who heed advice don't really need it, and those who need advice rarely heed it.

* * *

Advice is nice but example is ample.

* * *

There is no vice like bad advice!

* * *

When there are too many people giving instructions it becomes as confusing as using a dictionary for a roadmap.

* * *

Never tell somebody where to go unless you've been there!

* * *

Do people give away advice because they don't want it, or do they just have extra they don't need?

* * *

People don't like to be told they are wrong. In fact, they will sink to the lowest degree to prove that they are right, whether they are right or not!

* * *

Oh, how often our vain ambition leads to war and ammunition.

Memories

Absences make the heart grow fonder, but memories make the love last longer.

*   *   *

Memories are wasted when we forget to remember them.

*   *   *

Some of my dearest friends are memories. They never fail to help me unless I fail to remember them.

*   *   *

Dear Father,
I'm grateful for my memories
And the knowledge that I've gained,
The lessons teaching truth
Through experience and pain.
I'm grateful for my memory
So the memories remain,
That I don't have to repeat
These experiences again.
                    Amen.

*   *   *

Like a windy wheat field at harvest time
Or a golden summer sunset on the ocean,
Most of our memories are very closely
Related to emotion.

*   *   *

You can never find a better collection than in your mind, memory, and recollection.

Mistakes

We all make mistakes and fall down sometimes, but it's how we fall that's important. A skinned knee is a lot better than a broken leg, just as our wounded pride isn't as bad as a broken soul.

*   *   *

There are many times when I wish I could see into the future so that I might avoid mistakes. But then I realize that though I can see into the past, it seldom helps me to avoid mistakes. It does no good to want more when we don't use what we already have.

*   *   *

You can be too careful. When you avoid trying, in order to avoid mistakes, then you are being too careful.

*   *   *

Mistakes are made when we make decisions without using both our head and our heart.

Everyone makes mistakes, but wise is the man who can make them in such a way that he makes them look good.

*   *   *

Many stupid mistakes come as a result of a fear of asking stupid questions.

*   *   *

Stupid questions become stupid mistakes
when they're left unasked;
Questions are never stupid
if they help us perform the task.

*   *   *

When you stop trying, to avoid mistakes, then you're starting to make your biggest mistake.

*   *   *

Faith

We Owe God a Lot
An old man once said to me
That God owed him a lot
Because he lived his whole life true
And faith was all he sought.
I pitied the man who lived in vain
For the truth he never caught:

"For God sent his only begotten Son"
That our Eternal Lives were bought.

(from John 3:16)

*　*　*

Faith is sometimes believing things "common sense" tells us not to. That's because our conscience may not be properly trained. But faith is more powerful — it will train our conscience and strengthen our belief.

*　*　*

If someone doesn't understand, it does no good to look further. He would only see more to be confused about. A man can see no further then his own vision. Maybe we should just help him find out where he is.

31

I have found that my lack of Divine company doesn't result from ignoring His knock, and it doesn't result from leaving the door closed. It results from standing in the doorway and not moving out of the way so that He can enter.

*   *   *

Faith can move mountains, but only love can move people.

*   *   *

Lamps that are filled are not easily spilled.

*   *   *

One faith cannot be built from the destruction of another!

*   *   *

Our faith is like a triangle that points towards Heaven. The bottom line represents our faith in God. The two sides are our faith in ourselves and our faith in others. If any side is weak, the other two sides lack support and the whole entity is weak. If any part were left out, it would be pointless.

*   *   *

Before you can walk on water,
You must first walk through fire;
True faith must be preceded
By a burning desire.

Belief

People will be judged by what they believe,
Not by what we believe.
And we will be judged by what we believe
If we judge people.

*   *   *

Sometimes it's easier to die for our beliefs than to
live for them. Some fear life more than death. Don't
be afraid to live your beliefs. Don't be afraid to live.

*   *   *

Why do some of us believe we must give up our own
beliefs to believe another?

*   *   *

To a Rebellious Brother
I don't want to push you away by condemning your
sin, but I cannot push my beliefs away by condon-
ing it.

*   *   *

What do you stand for? Either you stand for the right
way or you stand right in the way.

*   *   *

You can't make belief from make-believe!

Hope

Since the beginning of time, and even today, there are two kinds of mystics in the world: The mystics of hope — optimistics, and the mystics of despair — pessimistics.

* * *

Most of my relationships can be described this way: So close and yet so far away.

* * *

Hope
There's nothing as tragic as a dying dream;
Nothing's harder to heal, nor harder to redeem.
But there is a magic, Hope it's said,
That heals the sick and redeems the dead.

* * *

Hope molds your dreams from a burning desire.
Keep your hope at work and your heart on fire.
When you let your dreams die, your hopes retire.

Religion

Religion is a way of life, and someone that doesn't have a way of life doesn't know how to live.

Religion is not a restriction to keep us from living the way that would make us happy. It is the key that grants us freedom, just as a kite is not restricted because of the string. The string keeps it soaring and prevents the kite from falling.

The Sabbath
The Sabbath is a day of rest,
Not a day of laziness.
Our body relaxes as our spirit works
On obtaining righteousness.

*   *   *

The falsest religion is that used to hide your true beliefs.

*   *   *

Unfortunately, with many people there is no difference between Theory and Theology.

*   *   *

There's a very big difference between "religious" and "righteous." One is the transportation, the other is the destination.

*   *   *

Conversion is the process of adoption.
To be a son of man or a son of God,
I must choose an option! (1 John, Chapter 3)

Righteousness

Sometimes we are the ripest when we are green.

*   *   *

Either you're a defender or you're an offender. There are no by-standers. (Matthew 12:30)

Those who don't abound in righteousness will be bound to something else they will never be free of. (John 8:32)

*   *   *

Just because the good side has bad guys doesn't make the bad side any better. It just gives the good side a bad reputation.

*   *   *

Even if the five foolish virgins had each owned oil wells their lamps would have been just as empty. It's not finding the oil, but filling our lamps which prepares us for the midnight when the bridegroom will come. (Matthew 25:1-13)

*   *   *

Jesus atoned for our sins. Yet sometimes we sin so often that we aren't attuned enough to take advantage of it.

*   *   *

Wheat And Tares
Wheat and tares come in pairs
And the only thing you can do
Is to live with each;
To practice and preach
The difference between the two,
And live to give,
Love and forgive
So that God will know which one is you.

Testimony

A soul is very fragile,
This fact I must defend;
An evil word, or act of hate
Could shatter one within.
A broken testimony
Is very hard to mend.

                *   *   *

A firm conviction will keep you cool during the heat
of friction.

                *   *   *

When we bear testimony we also bear the
responsibility of living the truths we declare.
Living a good example is letting our spirit bear
witness of the truth.

                *   *   *

Convictions with conditions are contradictions.

                *   *   *

Our testimony is a token of the truth that we've
sealed to our soul.

Feelings

Don't harbor harsh feelings —
Mend your wounds at the start
And you'll have faster healings.

*　　*　　*

Never overlook your feelings. Everything you feel
is real.

*　　*　　*

We should never use our convictions
To make others feel convicted,
But to make them feel convinced.

*　　*　　*

A man ashamed to show his feelings ought to be
ashamed.

*　　*　　*

There are two ways to hurt someone:
By causing pain, or by not stopping it.

Tears
Again they come, streaming down my face,
Tiny droplets of moisture, tears.
We are told we are weak who bear them,
But I think that's untrue.
It takes the stronger person
To let emotions through.
Those who dive into the depths of their soul
Stir up emotions that most have lost
In their fear of letting weakness show.
Now as my eyes fill with tears
I feel a sense of relief.
No matter what brings them to surface,
Joy, frustration, or grief,
These tears that come, I will not try to hide;
I know that my living well
Has not dried up inside.

*   *   *

Can they really know what you feel when you don't?

*   *   *

There comes a time when you have to put your foot
down. Just be careful not to stomp on anybody's toes
when you do so.

*   *   *

Be careful to be sharp and never cut. A dull mind
and a blunt statement can make the deepest wounds.

*   *   *

The mind has eyes but the heart has ears.

You say what you feel, but do you feel what you say?
Think about your feelings before you throw them
away.

*   *   *

Sometimes being left out in the cold is a better alter-
native than being burned in a heated discussion.

*   *   *

Never read people like you would a book;
It's easy to look over but it's easier to overlook!

*   *   *

Which is worse: subjection or rejection?

*   *   *

An ounce of pretension; a pound of unsure.

*   *   *

Follow your heart. It gives better directions than the
mind. The mind can rationalize, the heart cannot.
Your heart never lies!

*   *   *

So often, the expressions on our faces expose the
expressions in our hearts. Feelings, no matter how
deep they are buried, eventually rise to the surface.

*   *   *

You can never get used to getting used.

*   *   *

Don't let it go to your head until it has first gone to your heart!

*   *   *

When one is neglected, many suffer!

*   *   *

Maybe we should care less for what others think and care more for what they feel.

Fear

Sometimes we create our own demons.
Some are thought, some are fear, and some are doubt.
They're all very difficult to cast out.

*   *   *

Don't waste your life hiding in corners from your fears. Fear feeds upon your weakness in facing it and upon the strength you exhaust by hiding from it.

*   *   *

The fear of darkness many people have is not of being in the dark, but of being left in the dark.

The only man who has nothing to fear is the man who has nothing.

*　　*　　*

There are many people who will not try for fear of failure. They do not realize they have already failed. So much beauty is wasted when people avoid the rose because of the thorns.

*　　*　　*

It isn't because people are afraid of asking that they don't ask; it's because they are afraid of the answer.

*　　*　　*

A man who isn't afraid to face his fears is still afraid; he just doesn't want to stay that way.

*　　*　　*

Fear is what the coward and the courageous have in common; it's what they do about it that separates them.

Happiness

Try to be cheerful and not to worry.
Don't expect everything to go wrong.
Remember: men usually find what they're looking for.

*　　*　　*

Those who feel happiness only during the best of times will have a life of sorrow.

*   *   *

A smile is the sigh of the soul
expressing joy and love so
others might catch and continue the show.

*   *   *

Those who can't find happiness in this life will not find it in the next life either.

*   *   *

Is it the thirst or the drink that brings the most satisfaction?

*   *   *

People don't always know when they're happy, but they always know when they're not.

*   *   *

There's nothing more miserable than pretending to be something you're not, especially when you don't know what it is you want to be or what you are. Happiness cannot be pretended!

*   *   *

You are never truly happy until you can smile with your heart.

A smile is the nicest thing that can be said without speaking.

Humor

Someday I'm going to look back on all this and laugh. But it'll take a very long time to develop that kind of humor.

*   *   *

The sad thing about humor is that most people don't get it.

Joy

Remorse's tears stain the soul.

*   *   *

We should find things to enjoy in this life that won't take away from our joy in our next life.

Giving

If we can't give without expecting something in return, we don't have much to give anyway.

*   *   *

Those who give and don't expect, always get the most respect.

*   *   *

We can give in, give out, or give up.
Since there are so many ways to give,
Why don't we simply learn to give?

*   *   *

It does no good to give your 100% if you only give it 10% of the time.

*   *   *

The man will always have a lot
Who gives without a second thought,
But the man who doesn't think first
Will have the least and receive the worst.

*   *   *

Charity
I could speak as if an Angel
And have the Gift of Prophecy,
Or move mountains, as did Enoch
and understand all mysteries;
I could give all I own
To feed and clothe the poor,
Or let my body burn
for all that I've lived for;
But all these profit me nothing
If I have not Charity.
Because Charity suffereth long
and is not provoked easily.
Charity envieth not,
nor doth behave itself unseemly.
Charity is the pure love of Christ,
And two truths are contained within:
One is the pure love He has for us,
the other is our pure love for Him.
With these truths we can see
That of Faith, Hope and Charity,
Faith and Hope are only means
to the greatest of the Three.
(See I Corinthians Chapter 13)

*   *   *

After all that Jesus has given to me, all he wants in return is for me to show others what they have been given.

*   *   *

Would anyone have the same things they have now if they didn't have someone to share them with?

*   *   *

A generous man always has plenty to give, but a stingy man has nothing. If we won't share what we have then we really don't have anything anyway.

*   *   *

I believe a stingy man is a thief. After all, what is ours that has not been generously given to us? Those who will not share steal from Him who has given us everything.

*   *   *

Don't let people get the best of you; instead, give it to them.

*   *   *

Priceless is the man who can't be bought, and worthless is the man who can't give of himself freely.

Deeds

Acting depends upon action. If all our acts are good, we never have to act.

Bad actors result from doing repeat performances of a bad act.

* * *

It is a big misunderstanding that we should be rewarded for our accomplishments, because our accomplishments are the rewards.

* * *

It is the duty of man to do more than his duty, without robbing another man of his.

* * *

Works
By the debts that we owe,
By the greed that we show,
By the weeds that we grow,
By the seeds that we sow,
By our deeds He will know.

* * *

Sow what?

* * *

Everyone has a cheering section —
Silent and aloud,
But it's the act and the performance
That determines the size of the crowd.

* * *

Gratitude

Suicide is the ultimate ingratitude.

*   *   *

Without appreciation we experience depreciation.

*   *   *

A grudge is an investment where the interest earned
puts you further in debt.

*   *   *

With ingratitude we bite the hand that feeds us.

*   *   *

I'm grateful for those loved ones who have always
believed in me regardless of what I've believed.

*   *   *

People will do what you'd like them to,
If you like what they do for you.

Sacrifice

Sacrifice is only sacrifice when we do something
unwillingly.

*   *   *

Never sacrifice for something of little value.

*   *   *

Think of the things that we have to do that we dread and dislike — as an investment for greater things to come.

*   *   *

The disadvantage of taking advantage of something is that you have to pay for it later with interest.

*   *   *

Most people will sacrifice anything for a little pleasure but they won't sacrifice a little pleasure for anything.

*   *   *

Sacrifice isn't subtraction — lack of it is the substitution of satisfaction for salvation.

*   *   *

It's impossible to sacrifice at your convenience.

*   *   *

The thing to remember with blessings is "No deposit, no return."

*   *   *

Sacrifice seemed so hard at the start,
But who sacrificed the harder part:
The ritual sacrifice of the unblemished lamb
Or the actual sacrifice of the broken heart?

Service

He is much richer who has less money and serves the
Lord, than the man with lots of money who serves
himself.

*   *   *

Friendship is the deepest form of service.

*   *   *

We'd go a lot further if we'd go the extra mile for
others instead of trying to get extra mileage out of
them.

*   *   *

The man who serves himself receives a small serving.

*   *   *

You can't go the extra mile and take short cuts.

*   *   *

From the Lord's work
We're never retired.
We either labor or quit,
Or else we are fired;
"For unto whomsoever
much is given,
Of him shall be
much required."
   (Luke 8:48)

*   *   *

We cannot go the second mile until we have gone
the first.

*   *   *

Too many of us serve our fellow beings in the wrong
way. God never intended for us to make anyone our
idol.

Talents

A man's life is badly abused
When his talents are never used.

*   *   *

Talent is the cup we were all born with, but it's up
to us to fill it up.

*   *   *

There are lots of failures with talent, but there are
no winners without it.

Most everyone *has* talents, but only those who *use* their talents are the talented.

*   *   *

'Entertainment' is written on the headstones in the cemeteries of buried talents.

Willingness

Never allow yourself to become so divided that the portions are too small to work with.

*   *   *

How the truth fits into our lives depends upon the adjustments, alterations, and arrangements we make. Unfortunately, too many of us try to change the truth to fit our lives instead of changing our lives to fit the truth.

*   *   *

If the spirit is weak there's no telling what the flesh is willing to do!

God

We should never use our convictions
To make others feel convicted,
But to make them feel convinced.

* * *

When we study the creations we learn more about
the Creator.

* * *

Two of my greatest blessings are the knowledge of
my love for God and the knowledge of God's love
for me.

* * *

No one can exist without assistance!

* * *

"For with God nothing shall be impossible." Without
Him, everything is! (Luke 1:37)

If you could talk in person about your problems to
God, would you?

*   *   *

Without assistance, no one would exist; not even the
atheist!

*   *   *

The shortest distance between God and man is a
direct line of revelation, and the shortest distance
between Heaven and man is the straight and narrow
path in the Plan of Salvation.

*   *   *

I wonder how many events are called coincidence
when they really belong to providence? It only takes
a little common sense to know the difference and to
know the one with the real evidence.

*   *   *

Never provoke providence!

*   *   *

Through his divine investiture of authority
The truth is manifest,
But that does not suggest
That Heavenly Father is a ventriloquist;
Only that he will make no visitations
As an uninvited guest.

I wonder how often divine intervention has saved us from our foolish intentions, not to mention how often it has delivered us from our foolish inventions?

*   *   *

The Kingdom of God is always under construction,
Both from development and destruction.

*   *   *

God is the author of love and the author of our salvation. That's why we should study His word to build our testimony's foundation.

Holy Ghost

If you are uncomfortable with the way you live, it is because you do not live with the Comforter. (John 14:16-18)

*   *   *

We can't mix company spiritually.

*   *   *

The Gift of the Holy Ghost
Of all my gifts and presents
The one I need the most
Is the gift and precious presence
Of the Holy Ghost.

*   *   *

Be careful to which spirit you submit,
For there are only two:
The one that you can possess,
And the one that can possess you.

Jesus Christ

Let the example of the Savior be exemplified in our
behavior.

*   *   *

Spiritual Eclipses
Oh how dark our lives become
When the world blocks out
The light of the Son.

*   *   *

Jesus Christ truly was the manna-festation, the bread
of life. There is no manna as sweet as the bread of
life.

*   *   *

We cannot believe in his words until we first believe
in the Word. (John, Chapter 1)

*   *   *

There are too many people who study the letter of
the law instead of the spirit thereof. What is the letter
without the spirit? We cannot accept the truth unless
we accept its author.

You cannot believe in the Creator if you do not believe in his creations.

* * *

Sometimes I wonder if the Savior still suffers from our sins. Doesn't everyone?

* * *

Adam fell, but Christ picked us up. (1 Corinthians 15:25)

* * *

Where does the Son sit in Heaven? On the right hand of God.

* * *

Just Words
They're just words unless they're the words of the Word,
And they're just words until the Word is heard. (John, Chapter 1)

* * *

If you learn great things from great men, just think what you could learn from the one perfect man who walked this earth.

* * *

Don't worry, the yoke the Savior told us to take upon us has no cholesterol!

*   *   *

The Lamb of God
Mary had a little lamb;
The Lamb of God, behold;
He came to feed the flock of man,
For mankind was his fold.
He healed the sick and raised the dead;
He taught mankind to know
That everywhere the Good Shepherd led,
Man should always go.
"Come follow me," the Master said,
And as the scriptures all foretold,
Like a lamb to the slaughter He was led
And sacrificed to save his fold.
So we should strive to feed his sheep,
Like his Apostles all were told,
And his commandments we must keep,
To be numbered among his fold.

*   *   *

Jesus will come as a thief in the night and our righteousness will be the only alarm — the silent alarm of the Spirit.

*   *   *

It's amazing how many there are that cast stones at the only one without sin! (John 8:7)

*   *   *

Eat Light
Feast upon the words of Christ,
And develop an appetite.
Savor the flavor of the Savior
In every fulfilling bite.
And you can eat right,
Without eating lite.

*   *   *

Just think how creative we could become by studying the Creator.

Light

Just because everyone is doing wrong doesn't make it right. All the darkness of eternity cannot exceed the light.

*   *   *

Jesus said, "I am the light of the world." The light gets in everyone's eyes, but some it frightens, and others it enlightens. (John 8:12)

*   *   *

It is during the darkest times of our lives that we should most appreciate the Light.

*   *   *

There is a great difference between shining your light to blind and letting your light so shine.

A parable is light that casts shadows of obscurity on those who are unprepared to receive it, so that they will not be burned by the Light of Truth.

*   *   *

Those who stand on borrowed light trample it under their feet. (Matthew 7:6)

*   *   *

Without the light of the Son, we'd all be in the dark. (Luke 1:79, John 8:12)

Gospel

I'm often reminded that I should spend less time on the mysteries and more on the simple truths of the gospel. But I have learned that the lack of understanding is mystery, and usually a little time and study changes mystery into a simple truth. All the gospel is a mystery until we learn to understand it.

*   *   *

We are the figures.
Life's the equation.
The gospel is the answer.

*   *   *

It seems like there are too many limitations to what we can and can't do, and that we are bound by too many commandments. But if we were to do whatsoever we wanted without bounds we'd wander into condemnation and destruction. If it weren't for boundaries, what would separate Heaven from Hell?

*   *   *

Tithing
Most of my wealth is spent on living
Or squandered on worldly pleasures,
But I'm grateful, at least,
That one-tenth of my wealth
Is invested in heavenly treasures.

*   *   *

We can't receive the blessings of the Gospel unless we partake of its fruit. To partake is not merely to taste, but to consume completely. Too often we take a bite, then spit it out when the flavor's gone and thus gain no nourishment.

*   *   *

People need rules, not rulers!

*   *   *

There are no exact sciences or perfect systems other than the Plan of Salvation.

*   *   *

The scriptures are the assurance and the insurance, all in one.

*   *   *

The Gospel is spreading rapidly; "good news" travels fast.

*   *   *

We have to know the script
Before we can learn to act,
And the scriptures are the
Only script sure of fact.

                *   *   *

If the strait and narrow becomes winding or wide,
it's because you've wandered off to the side.

                *   *   *

Just think where we'd be if we would live the scriptures verbatim as we quote them.

                *   *   *

The scriptures are the best prescription, and
meditation is the best medication.

Prayer

It's amazing how the very act of praying many times
answers our own prayer.

                *   *   *

A prayer is the only long distance call we can make
for free.

                *   *   *

Forgetting our morning prayer is like forgetting to
wake up in the morning. Our spirit sleeps without
personal prayer.

It's a lot easier to have prayers in our thoughts than it is to have thoughts in our prayers.

* * *

Prayer is an example of the strength of the weak in searching for more strength.

* * *

God listens not to the words of your prayers until he has first heard the voice of your heart.

* * *

To Those Who Shout Prayers from Towers
Do not think that God
Cannot hear your silent prayer.
He's obviously not deaf
If he can hear us from up there.
Whisper your prayers
As quietly as you can,
For that is how Heavenly Father
Communicates to man.

* * *

A prayer is not a poem that must be recited word-perfect. It's a conversation with God and should be said freely and openly with the expression of our gratitude and necessities. Fancy words and decorated sentences only confuse communication. That is why the Savior taught that we should pray privately and not to be seen and heard of others.

Our Heavenly Father reads and hears our hearts
much clearer than our words. Our prayers just prove
that we are sincere enough to express what's in our
hearts.

*   *   *

Pointless Prayers
Praying to pray, just to get it out of the way
Is like talking without having anything to say,
Or like asking a question and then running away.

*   *   *

The Empty Prayer
"Why doesn't God answer me,
Does He no longer hear?
I repeat my prayer every day,
So carefully and clear."
Maybe God won't answer
If our prayer's insincere.

*   *   *

I go to bed, and as there I lay
I remember that I forgot to pray,
So I close my eyes like every day,
And fall asleep only half the way.
As morning comes and day is new,
I stop and think for a moment or two.
I wonder what good prayer would do
If God fell asleep half way through?

*   *   *

I've never felt the Spirit stronger anywhere
Than in the simple faith of a child's prayer.

*   *   *

Praying For Answers
Sometimes our problems seem so insignificant
That we don't think He'll understand,
But I think God, with all his wisdom
Knows and understands every thought of man,
And no problem is too small or big
To ask Heavenly Father for a hand.

*   *   *

When we neglect to pray we give our Heavenly
Father the silent treatment. He cannot help us if we
don't talk to Him.

*   *   *

Don't pray using vain repetitions. The Lord doesn't
like to be nagged either.

*   *   *

So often we kneel to pray
And ask God to show us the way,
Then we quickly finish and do not stay
To listen to what He has to say.
Instead, we mumble the same prayer like every day,
And then we rise and rudely walk away.

*   *   *

Sometimes I wonder if we aren't close enough for the Lord to hear or answer our prayers.

*   *   *

When our heart is troubled
With fear and doubt,
Like Daniel in the lion's den;
When all looks hopeless
And there's no way out,
Prayer's the best place to begin.

*   *   *

Prayer defies gravity so be careful what you pray for. If Heaven were to pour out everything we prayed for, most of our prayers would be very destructive.

Progression

Looking Back
Many of us are guilty of looking back
To some former sin or fault.
Yet we, unlike the wife of Lot,
Aren't changed into a pillar of salt.
This brings to mind what Jesus said,
And I read it with a nod:
"No man, having put his hand to the plough,
and looking back, is fit for the kingdom of God."
   (Genesis 19:26, Luke 9:62)

*   *   *

Seasons
Springtime flowers,
The fragrance of flowers:
The birds rejoice in the sky,
With beginning of life
And the joy of youth,
Life passes quickly by.
Summer breeze, dark green leaves,
The growing seasons wear on.
Life continues
And before you know,
Half the year is gone.
Autumn mountains, colored fountains,
Creating beauty from death;
The warmth leaves the countryside,
Replaced by Winter's breath.
Winter winds, life ends,
The snowfall blankets the earth;
Preparing the land and all therein,
For the fast-approaching rebirth.
Like the seasons, similar reasons
Apply to the life of men:
The beginning becomes the growing
And we grow until life ends —
To begin another season again.

*   *   *

Patience plus action equals persistence. Persistence
plus patience equals progression.

*   *   *

In climbing the ladder of life, be careful not to fall. But don't spend so much time being careful that you get hung up in the rungs.

*   *   *

The only proving I must do is improving.

*   *   *

There's a big difference between becoming perfect and becoming a perfectionist!

*   *   *

When all is said and done it will only have just begun.

*   *   *

What we don't want to become, we must overcome.

*   *   *

There are many who can't get past the past to catch up with the future.

*   *   *

Every destination is but a doorway to another, and every decision is another destination.

*   *   *

When we pause for applause, we interrupt the performance.

*   *   *

It seems like people only have two speeds: lethargic or fanatic, but steadfast is the only one that will get us to Heaven. (1 Corinthians 15:58, Colossians 2:5, Hebrews 3:14)

*   *   *

We'll always be what we are until we learn to be more or less.

*   *   *

There are no bottom lines as long as the story continues....

*   *   *

A shortsighted man will never see his long-range goals!

Gossip

Be careful with verbal attack,
Backbiting bites back.

*   *   *

Gossip is like gathering a lynch mob and crying murder against someone who is deaf and defenseless.

Watch out for a gossiper's attack.
Those fastest to your face
Are the fastest to your back.

*   *   *

Gossip is a lot like wine: it will not be sold before its time, and it goes through the grapevine so many times it's just as intoxicating.

*   *   *

There are many who don't aspire to the honors of men; instead, they conspire against them!

*   *   *

"To each, his own," is the answer to gossip and backbiting.

Comparison

We cannot bring comfort with comparisons, or by saying things will get better. If things were better, they would be better, and we can't bring comfort by saying things could be worse, because things are bad enough already. If things were worse, would they feel better? The only comfort we can bring is by comforting them with our love and understanding. Not in understanding that we know what they feel, because we only know what we feel, but in understanding that we know that they're hurting and we want to help them feel better.

Competition, comparison, and difference are the means people use to judge one another. If something is not what we are familiar with, we usually call it strange and incorrect without fully understanding what we are criticizing. It seems most people are competing to have more troubles than everyone else so they can judge others as being ungrateful that they aren't as bad off. We constantly compete for defeat to rationalize our failures, and for judgments of others by comparing.

*   *   *

Comparing crosses cripples our conviction.
You cannot compare crosses without a crucifixion.

Failure

Like attacking the enemy without planning a retreat,
Burning bridges is inviting defeat.

*   *   *

The fastest way to become a failure is to try and fulfill everyone's expectations.

Faultfinding

The expression: "You are what you eat" is especially true with faultfinding. It's a weak man who feeds on other people's weaknesses.

*   *   *

Those who burn others eventually suffocate from the smoke.

*   *   *

Why is it that someone can continue on and on with accusing hints, but when you confront him, he doesn't know what you're talking about?

*   *   *

I don't need anyone to tell me when I'm doing good; for there are plenty of people that will quickly tell me when I'm not.

*   *   *

It's too bad that the weaknesses of some people are pointed out when they point out the weaknesses in others, and that what they think is their greatest strength is sometimes their weakest point.

*   *   *

Everyone complains, but we don't have to prove it by complaining about the people who do!

*   *   *

You can't help someone find the truth by showing him his faults. An earthquake is more damaging than revealing.

Grudge

Life is heavy enough without carrying around a chip on our shoulder.

*   *   *

A grudge is an investment where the interest earned puts you further in debt.

*   *   *

The way to keep from getting a chip on your shoulder is by getting it off your chest.

*   *   *

Whenever I'm offended or feel a grudge developing, this formula helps to relieve the animosity: 70×7.

Human Interest

Don't ever believe you've figured someone out; that's impossible. People never know enough about themselves to give enough information to figure them out, and the information is always changing because people change. Besides, we have a lifetime to figure ourselves out, so why waste it trying to figure out others.

*   *   *

Those things we invest our hearts into are the most valuable of all. And any interest earned will compound for all eternity.

*   *   *

Isn't it amazing how people can be so close and so distant at the same time?

*   *   *

Never argue with someone who is defending himself personally. Too many people are losing that battle already. In this world of cynics, critics, and pessimists, we have to fight to stay on the right side of the lines.

* * *

Many people avoid getting to know others so that the goodbys aren't as painful, but is there more pain with goodbys than there is with no one to share your life and love with?

* * *

It costs but little effort to pay attention,
But it costs a lot more not to.

* * *

To Parents, Teachers, Preachers, and Employers: Intimidation is the poorest method of motivation.

* * *

Embarrassment is the inability to handle an uncomfortable situation.

* * *

Be not as the tree whose growth casts a shadow of burden on the growth of others; but rather, be as the tree whose shadow provides shade for comfort and protection.

Does a tough shell protect the tender heart or imprison it?

* * *

"I don't care" means "I need care."

* * *

Can people interact without making contact?

* * *

The harder it becomes to be original,
The easier it becomes to be predictable.

* * *

How many people are taking advantage of others in the attempt to avoid being taken advantage of?

* * *

Everyone's eyes tell a different story, some are interesting and some are boring.

* * *

On one touching occasion
Everyone cried,
Whether for joy or sadness
I can't decide.
And when it was all over
I also cried,
Because all I felt was empty inside.

Man holds the unfortunate distinction of being the primary species bringing other species to extinction.

*   *   *

As we learn humor and humility we learn the meaning of humanity.

*   *   *

To the world, prosperity is to posterity as popularity is to population. Too bad they can't see their true relation.

Appearance

If everyone were blind, everyone would be beautiful.

*   *   *

The attraction of the unattractive is in the uncommon ability to see its beauty.

*   *   *

There lived a beautiful woman
Long hair and fair skin,
But hatred and hypocrisy
Made her ugly within;
For her outward appearance
Was her only beautiful part.
You can't be truly beautiful
Unless you have a beautiful heart.

Anything of beauty becomes ugly when it is abused, and the most extreme abuse is simple neglect.

*   *   *

Isn't it frightening how closely fashion is related to passion.

*   *   *

It is sad how many of our customs involve costumes.

*   *   *

Have you ever noticed how many times the ugliest birds sing the prettiest songs? Everything has its beauty, but some just aren't as apparent as others. Their beauty comes from within, not without. Substance is always more appealing than surface, for sight is deceiving, appearances are illusions, and first impressions are obscure because "beauty is in the heart of the beholder."

Music

It's not how many songs we know or even what the song is about. It's feeling that you want to sing that counts.

*   *   *

The song doesn't matter if there's no harmony.

*   *   *

The only good stereo-types are those that play music.

Nature

Our Creator's Celestial Artwork

.
.
.
.
.
.   .

Nature is proof that God is an artist. Sunsets, sunrises, valleys, oceans, and all of God's handiwork are magnificent masterpieces of art. They are so touching to us because we are a part of it.

*   *   *

How can so many people believe that we are the result of evolution — an accidental freak of nature, when all of nature points to heaven and says, "There is a true and living God"?

*   *   *

The mighty river runs and runs for thousands of years,
and never runs out until man and engineers
begin to dump their problems into a solution
And poison and plague her with pollution.

Inspiration

You can't face the music when you're out of tune.

*   *   *

He who cannot follow directions will never have direction.

*   *   *

Aim is pointless without direction, and directions are aimless without a point.

*   *   *

Moments of rapture are either ruptured or captured.

*   *   *

Enlightening
The Spirit sparks your soul
With some unexpected cue;
Enlightening . . . striking
Like a bolt out of the blue —
An awakening and awareness
Like your body never knew.
Brainstorms and pain forms
Thoughts that rain on you,
And like the mind and the body,
The Spirit has its storms too.

*   *   *

Whether you count your blessings
Or you count your tribulations,
Your search will result in revelations.

*   *   *

Why is it that those who are out of tune are so soon immune? I guess even Eden unattended would turn to dune.

Contemplation

It's good to think about what you've been thinking. It's a way to communicate within yourself. Stop, ponder, and reason out what you've been thinking and what it means. You might call it "thought talk." That way you can talk out problems within yourself and find solutions, or solve problems before they begin and before you begin to take action.

There's an exception to every rule except exception.

*   *   *

A successful search requires research.

*   *   *

Everybody thinks, they just don't think about it.

*   *   *

A thing becomes a classic when it has no other classification.

*   *   *

A little thought always requires a lot more.

*   *   *

You're either making a bad mistake
Or else you're making a good start
If your decision causes a collision
Between your head and your heart.

*   *   *

We'll either look back on this and laugh, or we'll look back on this and bawl.
I guess it depends on whether we rise or we fall.
On second thought, maybe we shouldn't look back at all.

*   *   *

Imagination

I might not be able to travel through time or even afford to go to other countries, but with memories, dreams, imagination, and thoughts I can "mind travel" and go farther and a lot more often. Thought can take you anywhere you think.

*　　*　　*

Do angels have wings and halos?
Do demons have hooves and horns,
Or do men just have wild imaginations
Where fables and paganism are born?

Impression

Visitors
Impressions in my mind
Bring expressions all the time —
Feelings I can't ignore
Keep knocking on my door;
If I do they might not come anymore.

*　　*　　*

The pen is mightier than the sword because the stains of ink remain longer than the stains of blood.

*　　*　　*

Impressions
Many lives have engraven
their images in my heart,
And though they have
faded through the years
Their memories never depart.
For I can see clearly
through the tears in my eyes
That the feelings still remain,
and though the imprint's not as deep,
The impression's still the same.

Intelligence

Sometimes lack of perspective leads to deception. We are deceived by our own limited views which only allow a unilateral understanding of the truth. We can't understand anything completely until we have seen the complete picture. That's why perception results in deception.

*   *   *

Wisdom dresses in example,
Not in exclamation.
Ignorance becomes exposed
With too much explanation.

*   *   *

Intelligence is the ability to think without thinking about it.

*   *   *

The best annuity anyone could ever invest in is ingenuity.

Being intelligent is never having to prove it.

*   *   *

A man's greatest intelligence is in his understanding of another man's intelligence, and his greatest ignorance is in his lack of understanding of another man's ignorance.

Ignorance

Selfishness is the master of ignorance.

*   *   *

They are wise who know their ignorance.

*   *   *

You don't begin to learn until you begin to learn that you don't know it all.

*   *   *

People aren't fools, just foolish.

*   *   *

I have noticed that neither an ignorant man nor an intelligent man recognizes himself as such.

*   *   *

Ignorance has its advantages too; I just know what they are.

Which has killed more men, ignorance or education?

*   *   *

Sometimes ignorance is the knowledge of things we don't need to know but learn anyway.

*   *   *

Someone has to be very dense if he can't see evidence of providence!

*   *   *

At first I thought...but then I thought.

*   *   *

Thinking isn't difficult. It's learning to control your thoughts that's hard. However, it's much easier to control your thoughts than to live with them if you don't.

*   *   *

It's amazing how the mind can be so hard at work doing nothing.

*   *   *

Thought can be very distracting.

*   *   *

He thinks twice as fast who thinks twice as much.

If we would think twice about everything we did
we'd probably think twice as much as we do, and
we could probably do twice as much as we think and
we'd probably do only half as much as we have done.

*   *   *

Lectures and lessons have seldom taught
The truth within a simple thought.

*   *   *

Isn't it amazing how a little thought can fill your
mind?

*   *   *

A thought is never a waste of time as long as it
entertains or brings us peace of mind.

*   *   *

A man has truly been taught
If his thoughts have feelings
And his feelings have thought.

*   *   *

As I pour out my thoughts in evaluation, many
thoughts escape from evaporation.

*   *   *

Whether you're a hostage or you're a host,
Depends if you're in control or if you coast
And upon the thoughts you entertain the most.

"As a man thinketh in his heart, so is he;"
A man's heart is his legacy.
A man's thoughts are prophecy.
"As a man thinketh in his heart" is destiny.
   (See Proverbs 23:7)

*   *   *

Thoughts and Feelings
It's hard to tell which will provide the best
protection,
But your head will never steer you wrong
If your heart's pointed in the right direction.

*   *   *

A good way to know if your thoughts are pure is to
ask yourself what you know, and how you know for
sure.

Wisdom

He who stays on his toes stands a little taller.

*   *   *

It is said that genius is the ability to remember
everything you learn, but I say that true genius is
the ability to apply what you learn.

*   *   *

The mind is cheap to feed but costly to fill.

If a man's earning capacity is equal to his learning
capacity, he's probably poor.

*   *   *

What good is it to make up your mind if you don't
know what it is made of?

*   *   *

A man is always in a bind if his tongue is quicker
than his mind.

Justice

Most people would O.D. on just the smallest dose of their own medicine.

*   *   *

If the wrong didn't have rights, what difference would there be between the wrong and the right?

Equality

There is equality in talents and trials. Where there is a weakness in one area, there is compensation in another.

*   *   *

If all men were created equal, why do men create inequality?

*   *   *

As long as men will try to see eye to eye, they will not esteem themselves above another. They will see themselves as equals.

*   *   *

Just think of what could be accomplished if men would strive for equality instead of trying to get even.

Free Agency

Isn't it ironic that God gives men their free agency, And they use it to take it away from other men.

*   *   *

God has given us free agency, but it does us no good if we don't give it back.

*   *   *

Free Agency
Every person is free
To choose his own destiny,
And determine what he'll be
Throughout all eternity.
Our most valuable gift is free,
To use it's the only fee.
This gift to humanity
Is called Free Agency.

*   *   *

What we have in store for us depends on how we shop.

Judgment

Can it be held against you if you never held it?

*   *   *

When we confuse conjunction with conclusion the result is often confusion.

*   *   *

"The last shall be first and the first shall be last," and at last there shall be no more cutting in line.
    (Matthew 20:16)

*   *   *

Neither the wicked nor the righteous shall be plucked until they are fully ripe. (Matthew 13:24-43)

*   *   *

May all our misjudgments of others be in favor of good!

*   *   *

After this life, there will come a time when we will have to confess our sins that we haven't repented of, and we will be our own prosecutor and judge. You cannot plead the 5th on Judgment Day.

*   *   *

I have never supported suicide.
In fact, it's a fate
I could never comprehend.
But maybe these despairing souls decide
They fear the judgments of God
less than the judgments of men.

*   *   *

You have the right to remain silent. Everything you say can and will be held against you at the Judgment Seat of Christ.

Judging

People will be judged by what they believe,
Not by what we believe,
And we will be judged by what we believe
If we judge people.

*   *   *

We have the right to judge but not to pass judgment. We have to judge to discern between good and evil, but it is for ourselves, not others.

*   *   *

Those who look down on others are in the lower position.

*   *   *

If excuses were the evidence of our failures we'd all convict ourselves.

To judge a man by his actions is to measure the
stature of a man by his shadow without taking into
account the light. What we see depends primarily
on where we are.

*   *   *

Unrighteous Judgment
I often think of the heroes
Long since dead and gone,
Men like Benedict Arnold
Who are remembered for their wrong.
I have read of King David's fall,
And the mistake that Samson made.
Why do we mortals dwell on the bad
And leave the good to die and fade?
As I reflect upon their lives
There comes to mind a sobering thought:
Wasn't it with the blood of Christ
The sins of mankind were bought,
So who are we the puny man
To judge them and condemn;
How can we be so sure
God hasn't forgiven them?

Liberty

After only a few decades of decadence, men will
literally destroy their own liberty with their liberality.

*   *   *

There's only one way to be free of captivity —
"Ye shall know the truth and the truth
shall make you free." (John 8:32)
Never wave the white flag, whatever you do, or you'll
surrender the red, white, and blue.

Unity

There are too many fences in the world. People are
putting up fences to keep out the neighbor kids, or
pets, and separate themselves from the community.
We put up defenses to make sure we are never
wrongly accused. People could be so much closer if
there weren't so many barricades separating them.

*   *   *

Just think of the unity if everyone had as much desire
to be equal as they did to be superior.

Life

Life is:
Leaving and receiving,
Arriving and surviving,
Giving and forgiving,
Learning and returning.

*   *   *

Life is heavy enough without carrying a chip around
on our shoulder.

*   *   *

We are the figures.
Life's the equation.
The gospel is the answer.

*   *   *

Those who cannot find happiness in this life will not
find it in the next life either.

*   *   *

You haven't seen the whole picture until you've seen the background too.

*   *   *

No matter what kind of mark we make in this life there will be those who misinterpret it as graffiti. What's important is that our mark is recorded in the Lamb's Book of Life where it is translated correctly by the Savior. (Revelation 3:5; 13:8)

*   *   *

If time is your friend, life is your family.

*   *   *

Life is a test of our responsibility. If we can't handle the keys to our own house, we can't expect keys to our own mansion.

*   *   *

Don't let the flowers you've put on a loved one's grave
Be the only flowers you ever gave!

*   *   *

May your days go on and on,
And may you live them one by one.

*   *   *

Drugs are the diet of death. Poison in moderation only kills more slowly!

God is the accountant,
Life is the account,
And we are accountable.

*   *   *

There's a little of the past
In everything I see.
The present is made up of
Bits of history,
And the future is what
We are building presently.

*   *   *

What we live is what we give in return for life.

Eternal Life

God has given us the greatest gift
And we will never be able to repay,
But we can try by accepting his gift
And not throwing it away.

*   *   *

Many of us would rather pave our own road to
destruction than stay on the strait and narrow path
that leads to salvation. Some sacrifice everything for
nothing; others sacrifice nothing for everything. It's
amazing what people will do to get their own way
regardless of where it takes them.

*   *   *

What will we do with eternal life if we can't even manage this one?

*   *   *

"This is life eternal, that they may know thee, the only true God, and Jesus Christ, whom thou hast sent." (John 17:3) You know where you are by the distance in your relationship.

*   *   *

Prominence is never permanence, but it is often a hindrance to our eternal inheritance.

Future

Those who don't learn to prepare,
Learn to repair or they learn to despair.

*   *   *

Time invested in the future is never a waste.

Heaven/Hell

Heaven is a magnificent place.
We don't have to worry about seeing
Our enemies there;
Of course we'll never get there
If we have enemies.

*   *   *

They abundantly live that easily forgive.

*   *   *

As soon as we begin to comprehend Heaven we become a part of it. The amount we become depends upon the amount we comprehend.

*   *   *

There is no hell as bitter as the gall of loneliness.

*   *   *

Those who go to hell are not strangers to it. They have visited it enough to know what to expect.

*   *   *

Neither heaven nor hell is ever the same for any two people.

*   *   *

I think that someday, after time dissolves the mysteries of life and death, we will find that heaven was never very far away and that those who didn't find it had their attention on something else instead.

*   *   *

Heaven can wait, but hell is impatient.

*   *   *

We cannot get into the Kingdom of God with reservations!

*   *   *

He lived his life —
Or at least he tried,
To make others happy he lived
And not sorry he died.
Now he continues to live,
Completely satisfied,
Making others happy he lives
On the other side.

*   *   *

You can't go nowhere, but you can go somewhere worse!

*   *   *

My definition of heaven is having my Heavenly Father say to me, "This is my beloved son in whom I am well pleased."

*   *   *

Heaven is just like earth—it's not what you know but who you know that will get you there. (John 17:3)

*   *   *

There is no government in heaven or on earth that doesn't use some kind of pyramid structure to regulate and direct its administration.

Those who understand the principles
Of opposition and progression well
Would probably be the first to tell
That Eden could not be like heaven
Any more than it could be like hell.

*   *   *

There is a small veil between heaven and hell, and
it is called, "I meant well."

*   *   *

The kingdoms of heaven and hell are like a lifeguard
and a drowning victim — whether they're saved or
they're damned, they take someone with them.

*   *   *

Some people have to have the hell scared out them
before they will start thinking about heaven.

Time/Eternity

I believe that the two stupidest statements
I have ever heard are
I can't afford to save money and
I haven't got time to be religious.

*   *   *

I've found that time becomes more meaningful and
useful when I'm not "watch watching."

The beginning is a beginning to the end,
And the end is the beginning again —
A cycle that will always be
One eternal history.

*   *   *

Tomorrows are just yesterdays continuing todays —
Eternity broken down into endless time delays,
An ongoing cycle of time replenishing the days.

*   *   *

The Human Race
So little time to perfect our soul,
We race the clock to reach our goal.

*   *   *

You can take your time, just don't take someone else's!

Love

Building the Basics
It does no good to vote if there isn't an election,
It does no good to reach if it's in the wrong direction,
It does no good to love if we cannot show affection.

* * *

It's a weak love that can't be expressed. When we really love someone we want to share that love. It doesn't matter if it's our grandparents, parents, children, wives, friends, or our Heavenly Father. If we love them we will want to share it by expressing our love in statements, testimonies, prayers, and example. Telling others we love them is not difficult unless there is nothing to tell.

* * *

Touch is a small part of affection,
Just as contact is incomplete connection.
Touch brings pleasure to the skin,
But love only lasts if touched within.

True love is a heart bursting with love, and yet enough emptiness for more love to grow.

*   *   *

"I love you" is the most anyone can say in one sentence.

*   *   *

Love is the only thing that you can show off and benefit others.

*   *   *

If love is blind, no wonder sight is so deceiving.

*   *   *

It's amazing how love allows someone to see in another what no one else can see.

*   *   *

Amount of Love
It's not the amount you learn
Or the amount you know,
Rather it's the amount you live,
And the amount you love
That amounts the most
To our Father above.

*   *   *

Charity
It is unfortunate that men have to be at their lowest
level of despair before they become aware of the
highest order of love.

*   *   *

If we spent our life like we spent our money, just
think how enriched the world would be.

*   *   *

Love is more important than life or death.

*   *   *

A heart that has been expanded with love will never
return to its original shape.

*   *   *

Does every story have to be a parable of profound
analogy, or a proverb or metaphor with some hidden
message to be searched, studied, and scrutinized to
find its moral? Can't there be just one straightfor-
ward song, story, or poem with a simple but yet
profound truth that means the same regardless of
who or what you are? One like, "I love you!"

*   *   *

Affection can both cure and cause infection!

Love is the most profound word in the English language and the most powerful force of all. No other word has nearly as much meaning or importance. It was because of love that our Heavenly Father sent his only begotten son, and Jesus's life was a message of love for mankind. Life is the proof of God's love.

*   *   *

Your head is never too big as long as your heart is bigger.

*   *   *

To say "I love you" is a lot easier than to show it;
Live your love so that they will always know it.

*   *   *

What good is a love poem that's unromantic,
When you can't understand it because of the semantics?

*   *   *

The shortest love poem,
But the one most true
Has only three words:
"I love you."

*   *   *

The Conjunction
Our hearts aligned —
Two orbs combined
To become one orbit —
The conjunction.
Love, the gravity —
The energy
That controls the function.

Compassion

We don't have to have done something wrong to feel sorrow.

*   *   *

It's a strong man who can live a hard life without his heart hardening also.

*   *   *

An apathetic man is a pathetic man.

*   *   *

I'm saddened to think that some have chosen to let others care for their parents. What if they had let others take care of us? Are they too much trouble when they become unable to take care of themselves because of their age? I cannot possibly imagine giving my baby away because she can't take care of herself. Does age change our love for our loved ones? Does our love age with age?

If our compassion for something depends upon our judgment of its intelligence, then we are neither very intelligent nor compassionate.

* * *

You can be too careful but you can't be too full of care.

* * *

If everyone could actually see through someone else's eyes for just one day, we'd never see the same nor be the same again.

Kindness

When we say something stupid we should shut up. After all, it's not polite to talk with your mouth full.

* * *

People should try to be more timid and less intimidating.

* * *

It's good to give long thought before speaking. Make sure your words are helpful and not hurtful. Sometimes, whether we realize it or not, we say things that hurt. If we would just think for a moment of what we are going to say or how it could be interpreted, we might make a compliment instead of a thoughtless comment or complaint.

You should always treat people better even if they're not. People are always better if we treat them that way.

*   *   *

How sad that I would ever
Push their love away
By paying no attention
To the things they have to say.
Yet how often I tear
Their tender hearts from mine
By neglecting to give them
Just a little of my time.

*   *   *

Is it rude to interrupt someone when he is talking to himself?

*   *   *

Sometimes, a lack of praise is the cruelest punishment.

*   *   *

Kindness is like an avalanche — it starts with one small action. It doesn't take a lot of effort to cause a chain reaction.

Opposition

Everybody has a certain amount of wants, won'ts, and woes in their life. There are certain things we want whether we need them or not. There are certain things we won't do whether we are supposed to or not, and there are certain amounts of woes that will result whether we want them or not.

*   *   *

In between our times of suffering come most of our greatest times. They are created by our suffering to help us overcome it. Our suffering actually gives us the strength to overcome it.

*   *   *

Even though we sometimes get tired of the constant force against us, without this opposition we wouldn't survive long. As soon as we stop swimming against the current and allow ourselves to flow with the tide, we become too weak to continue. As hard as it may seem, the struggle to exist gives us the strength to do so, and to survive we must swim upstream. Dead things float downstream.

*   *   *

From gospel hymn to gossip song — how short the distance between right and wrong.

*   *   *

Adversity is not of the Adversary, but of the Advocate.

*   *   *

Opposition is the only thing with no opposite.

*   *   *

The path of least resistance only spreads the opposition over a longer distance.

*   *   *

In life's ups and downs, highs and lows, everyone prefers the higher elevation; however, we could not enjoy or appreciate it without the view of its opposite.

*   *   *

The purpose of an obstacle course is to go over the obstacles, not around them. Going over them is the only way to get over them.

Opposition bears the twins of darkness and light, of good and evil that must remain with us throughout our life. However, opportunity allows us the agency to choose which one we will nurture and raise.

*   *   *

Opposition is priceless to our progression. Remember the coin has no value without both sides.

*   *   *

Obstacles either obstruct or instruct.

*   *   *

Storms
There's been no rain for a month or two,
The earth's in pain and the sky is blue.
Storms shower all life to refresh and renew.
A cloud in the sky — a tear in the eye,
It's amazing what a little moisture can do.

*   *   *

Mathematics
I know that everything has its opposition,
But I'm more interested in a positive mission.
Negative and positive can play the opposite position,
But try to imagine and envision
Life with less subtraction and division
And more multiplication and addition.

Discouragement

Don't be discouraged if you're not very popular,
Neither was Jesus when he lived on the Earth.

*   *   *

Sometimes we think it's not in the cards, when what
we ought to do is reshuffle the deck.

*   *   *

Since the beginning of time, and even today, there
are two kinds of mystics in the world — the mystics
of hope: optimistics, and the mystics of despair:
pessimistics.

*   *   *

Sometimes I receive so many injuries from the
punishments I inflict upon myself, for not doing as
good as I'd like to, that I lack the strength to do
better.

*   *   *

Depression is the darkest shade of blue.

*   *   *

Tours of pleasure are detours from happiness.

*   *   *

People without hope are easy prey for despair.
Beware: despair is the hardest damage to repair!

*   *   *

When you are on the edge is not a good time for
sightseeing; it's a good time for watching your step.

*   *   *

If you are under the weather, stay out of the storm!

*   *   *

The fastest road to misery is to try and fill everyone's
expectations. Everyone's expecting; let them make
their own deliveries!

*   *   *

If you knew it wouldn't work, you planned it that
way.

*   *   *

It's a small world unless you are traveling or lonely.

*   *   *

Discouragement
Satan has no power strong enough
To make me give in,
But oh how easy a little discouragement
Can get me to give up and let him win.

Everyone gets discouraged and tells themselves,
"I quit," but only the foolish really listen to it.

*   *   *

When you're at the end of your straw
Will you win, lose, or draw?

Problems

We can't solve a problem by blaming others, and we
can't delegate a problem. Giving away the blame
won't ease the pain. The only way to solve a problem is to realize its existence and then work on its
extinction.

*   *   *

Most of our questions contain a part of the answers
to our problems.

*   *   *

Avoidance is the acquaintance of new problems with
the old ones.

*   *   *

Most of our problems come from allowing them
to exist.

*   *   *

Those who swim in the streams of extremes drown
in the currents of simplicity.

Those who concentrate too hard on not getting stung often walk right into the hornet's nest. If you turn all your attention to what might happen, you don't notice what's happening.

*   *   *

Our problems are a part of the solution. Unfortunately, our solutions are the largest part of the problem.

*   *   *

The pressure is never too great when the weight is equally distributed.

*   *   *

Isn't it amazing how many problems we create, making sure our problems are real.

*   *   *

You can't have a brainstorm with a clouded mind.

*   *   *

My biggest problem is not knowing what my problem is, and my second biggest problem is knowing my problems too well.

*   *   *

When you have more solutions than problems, you have more problems.

Those who don't recognize the problem are often a part of it.

*   *   *

You have problems when everyone knows your problem but you.

*   *   *

There are two ways to approach any obstacle: carefully or carelessly.

*   *   *

Reason is not always the answer, but it is often the problem.

*   *   *

It's been said that if everyone's troubles were placed in one large pile, we'd each take our own, but I think I'd be content just to leave mine there.

*   *   *

When your only cause is because, you're probably only causing problems.

*   *   *

Problems arise when we criticize, and the problems grow worse while the critics converse.

*   *   *

Your problems will always exist if you don't leave them exits.

* * *

There are two ways to handle the problems that are eating at you: starve them or stuff them.

* * *

Facing life's problems is what it's all about.
We face them with hope, or we face them with
    doubt.
We either learn to cope, or we learn to cop out.

Worry

There are too many people who are bothered by nothing.

* * *

The man who can't be lazy once in a while is not a hard worker!

* * *

A lot of times the dam is more trouble than the flood.

* * *

If you bite off more than you can chew, don't swallow!

"Don't worry" is the most useless advice and yet the most needed.

*   *   *

We just have to worry about getting it together; there are plenty of people who will tell us where to put it.

*   *   *

Worry
Worry is like still water
On the seeds of trouble:
The roots grow deep
And the problems double.
And worry is like a rushing current
On the seeds of peace:
The seeds are washed away
And troubles increase.

Peace/War

Those who live with anxiety most of the time
Feel uneasy with serenity.

* * *

The only peace of mind some have is that inside their head.

* * *

I can't understand it. Countries are at war, families are being separated because of divorce, people are constantly suing one another over everything. It seems everyone is at each other's throat when they should be hugging their neck.

* * *

As long as there are prisoners of war, the war continues.

* * *

Peace comes not by concentrating on it, but by letting it concentrate on you.

* * *

To prepare for peace is the most effective way of preventing war.

* * *

Let the chips fall where they may, but be sure to get out of their way.

* * *

By good will to men, good men will win.

* * *

I never feel better by giving someone a piece of my mind. I can't afford to lose either one: my peace of mind or a piece of my mind!

* * *

Never speak your piece when your heart's at war!

* * *

When the world's more concerned with warfare than welfare then we can bid the world farewell.

* * *

He was at war with himself; he had no peace of mind!

*   *   *

For peace: be still.

*   *   *

All the lead ever discharged through weapons of war is not near as lethal as the lead used as ammunition in the hands of the wrong writer!

*   *   *

Paci-Fist
A Pacifist fights behind the lines
Of a battle where armies cannot go.
And even though the war
Is more silent and less violent,
He delivers just as powerful a blow.

Contention

Inventions of contentions often begin with good intentions.

*   *   *

It takes two to argue and two to contend;
If only one argues the argument ends.
At least two must contend
Or the spirit of contention will not attend.

Arguing religion is like playing football in a mine field: there are more casualties than points made in the confrontation.

*   *   *

If you feel like a bartender at an A.A. convention, it's probably because you're serving and drinking with the spirit of contention.

Enemies

Never underestimate the power of your foe! The germ has killed more men than any other beast!

*   *   *

Men that can't learn from their enemies won't last long!

Relationships

People are without friends because
They're unfriendly to others.
Be friendly and you'll have friends.

*   *   *

The development of a relationship comes from our
ability to relate our feelings with one another.

*   *   *

Never trust a man who never feels guilty, or one who
always does.

*   *   *

Be not as the tree whose growth casts a shadow of
burden on the growth of others; be as the tree whose
shadow provides shade for comfort and protection.

*   *   *

It's frightening how alone two people can be together when they don't understand each other.

*   *   *

Those who are never offended never have to defend themselves.

*   *   *

Just because we are related doesn't mean we relate.

*   *   *

"No pain, no gain" especially applies to relationships.

*   *   *

You can learn more about someone in an hour of crisis than you can from years of acquaintance.

*   *   *

Most of my relationships can be described this way: So close and yet so far away.

*   *   *

Relationships become long distant when there are too few direct calls. Relationships should be more person to person.

*   *   *

We will always be alone until we start
To make our heart a home in someone else's heart.

*   *   *

Trust is a greater discipline than punishment.

*   *   *

There is entirely too much footwork between people.
Too often we think we have to kiss someone's feet to
keep from stepping on them. But if you stay on your
toes you can stand your own ground without
stepping on other people's toes or kissing their feet.

*   *   *

If we realized just how we come across, we'd
probably cross fewer people.

Communication

In the tactics of speech, if one isn't tactful, he's tacky.

*   *   *

The only thing that is really unfair is the miscon-
ception that everything should be fair.

*   *   *

The shortest distance between two viewpoints is a
straight line of communication.

Suggestion is the art of answering the question while asking it.

*   *   *

There are many times when silence is more profound than speech!

*   *   *

Exaggeration is the ability of using enough adjectives to stretch a black and white event into a large, colorful adventure without turning it into a white lie or a discolored fairy tale.

*   *   *

There is never enough conservation of conversation.

*   *   *

People don't complain because they have something to say. They complain because they want to be heard.

*   *   *

Silence, once broken, is hard to replace.

*   *   *

A smile is the nicest thing that can be said without speaking.

*   *   *

Speaking, unlike writing, should only be done in first person.

Compromise

It's easy to compromise principles. Many of us consider going the extra mile as going a half mile forward and a half mile back.

*   *   *

Any concept carried into the courts of controversy is seldom settled with a sentence of conversion.

*   *   *

There's a big difference between compromising and improvising.

Family

When I was young, I thought parents knew everything; now that I'm a parent, I know they don't. It's a good thing children don't know what parents know!

*   *   *

It's funny that adults can be more childish than children.

*   *   *

The family is God's strongest army. What other unit of power has better withstood and conquered evil?

*   *   *

How can one measure the tremendous love that is shared in the worry of concerned parents over their small sick child?

*   *   *

If there is any truth to the concept that we are the products of our environment, then I can understand all the more the importance of the home!

*   *   *

The Man and the Woman
The man — "the firstborn of Mother Earth,"
content in his ignorance,
his curiosity ignited with his new world,
had no mind to disobey.
But the woman — "the mother of all living,"
discontent with the loneliness
of an empty womb, disobeyed.
Partaking of destiny
that man might be,
and then as castouts, cursed with death,
The man and woman set about
obeying their highest command —
"To multiply and replenish the earth."

*   *   *

You can fix the holes in your home
When they're in walls and in ceilings,
But the holes in the home that are hard to repair
Are holes found in hearts and in feelings.

*   *   *

The rewards of being a parent aren't always apparent until the child becomes a parent.

*   *   *

How can we find sanctity unless our homes become a sanctuary?

*   *   *

Signs
Children are not blind.
They can see
When our heart reads
"No Vacancy."

Friendship

Friendship is a special love that enables us to examine and explore the hearts of others so that we can understand our own.

*   *   *

Friendship is the truest service of fellowship.

Marriage

Marriage is the picking up from where our parents left off in raising children, and continuing the process.

*   *   *

The problem with marriage today is that too many people think of marriage vows as just words, and not as covenants and commitments. They think of them as vowels instead of vows.

*   *   *

A good babysitter will help a marriage more than any marriage counselor.

Repentance

We are more righteous when we realize we need to repent.

*   *   *

From prodigal to prodigy,
This parable applies so perfectly;
Those who learn their lesson well,
Learn to repent instead of rebel.

*   *   *

It's far easier to find solutions than absolutions!

*   *   *

We are all prodigal, for sin leads us astray,
But repentance sends us back on our way.

*   *   *

You can only repent once for a sin. You never really repented if you have to do it again.

One in every ninety and nine is a prodigal son awaiting his time.

*   *   *

A Father's Reflections for a Wayward Son
My son, my son, why hast thou forsaken me?
It was thy will, not mine, that caused this to be,
I can't look upon sin with the least degree,
Please repent, my son, and come back to me.
I have provided a Shepherd to guide my sheep.
Now my son, do not stray. We can stay
Together for all eternity,
As father and son with all our family.

*   *   *

A sin takes a long time to finish. It's not over until we've repented.

*   *   *

Repentance gives us a chance to do it all again, as long as we don't repeat any of our past transgressions and sins.

*   *   *

Men are angry because of the admonitions of the Lord, and the Lord is angry because of the abominations of men. If we'd repent of our sins our relationship would mend, and love would develop and the anger would end.

*   *   *

Though your crosses seem unbearable,
Your sins are not so terrible
That your life is unrepairable.

*   *   *

No one should have any regrets who believes in repentance.

*   *   *

Man repents at Christ's expense;
That's the divine commission of recompense.

Change

Sometimes making the change from today to tomorrow can be a very expensive transaction.

*   *   *

How many of us kneel at the altar of alternatives but never change our ways?

Conscience

Our conscience blurs when rationalization occurs.

*   *   *

Man can only follow one force.
He can only heed one voice:
Either pride or conscience, never both.
He has to make a choice.

No one can give you better advice than your conscience.

*   *   *

Our conscience is our own personal lie-detector.

*   *   *

When you do something wrong and it doesn't bother you, it should really bother you.

Forgiveness

In this life we experience a bit of heaven and a bit of hell. We get a little taste of what the next life will be like, depending on how we live and think. To some, this life will be the only heaven they will know, and to some it will be the only hell they will ever know.

*   *   *

When others are doing wrong we shouldn't do worse to try and make it right. It is foolish to stray from the strait and narrow path just because others are out of line.

*   *   *

Without the possibility and ability to forget all men would be evil geniuses.

*   *   *

Forgetting is just as important as remembering. Even
God in his infinite wisdom, forgets sometimes.

*   *   *

When you forgive and forget,
Think of the interest you earn,
You give your anger away
And get their love in return.

*   *   *

Those who cannot forgive others are always
offended.

*   *   *

It's easy to forgive and forget
the offense against you made,
but it's difficult to forget
the offense that you forgave.

Guilt

Guilt is a personal atonement for committing sin,
removed only by repentance. It is a reminder of how
Jesus Christ felt as he atoned for our sins.

*   *   *

A man is not innocent just because he can reveal the
faults of others while concealing his own; he is just
better at hiding his guilt.

No earthquake ever admits his own fault in a disaster.

* * *

Being bad sometimes feels good but it never feels right!

* * *

Guilt is the idiot-light of the soul. It tells us when something is wrong so that we can repair the damage before our soul is destroyed.

Humility

Humility
Those who are most gifted,
Of themselves they never boast,
The greatest gift, "Humility,"
The gifted seek the most.

* * *

Humility is the ability
To conquer vanity
With, and in spite of
Humanity. (Romans 12:21)

* * *

Humility is the ability of lowering yourself to a greater position.

* * *

Humility is the proof that some things are better concealed than revealed.

*　*　*

Humility is the ability of concealing both.

*　*　*

Someone who can say "I may be wrong" is usually right.

*　*　*

Humility is an interesting concept. When we disguise our faith through humility, we advertise our faith with example.

*　*　*

The greatest strength of any man is knowing when to reveal it and when to conceal it.

*　*　*

Humility is the only way we can get low enough to see there is no one beneath us.

*　*　*

Humility is an interesting principle. Only in the depths of humility can we reach the lofty heights of faith. Many times I've stumbled and been humbled, but I never stay there long enough to get anywhere.

Is it possible to be humble without being humbled?

*   *   *

No one ever gets fat on humble pie because you don't
have to swallow much pride to spoil your appetite.
It's true: you can't have your cake and eat it too.

Responsibility

Can they be held responsible who have not been taught responsibility?

* * *

The worst thing about being responsible is that everything becomes your responsibility.

* * *

Are we responsible if we are irresponsible?

* * *

If you know when to hurry and when to wait, you'll either be early or else you'll be late.

* * *

We can't get anything out of life if we try to get out of everything.

* * *

Jonah was a good example of how running from our responsibilities only gets us in deep water!

* * *

He is more crippled who cannot stand on his own two feet than he who does not have feet!

* * *

Sometimes irresponsibility comes by not accepting responsibility.

* * *

Vengeance is never a victory to a victim.

Debt

I believe that the two stupidest statements
I have ever heard are:
I can't afford to save money, and
I haven't got time to be religious.

* * *

Only a foolish man buys expensive aspirin for headaches caused by debt.

* * *

Oh that I might budget my income so that my "Book of Life" has no Chapter 11.

It is one thing to spend money on a poor book, but it is far worse to waste your time and mind on it.

Entertainment

"R and R" doesn't stand for retirement and relegation.

* * *

Why do entertainment and education have such a distant relationship?

Idleness

Idle hands are calloused from the labors of misdeeds.

* * *

Fate is for those who are too lazy to define their own destiny.

* * *

Only the sweat of our brow can wash away the poison of idleness.

* * *

It's amazing how many people confuse being comforted with being comfortable.

* * *

Boredom visits everyone, but it lives with those who are idle.

*   *   *

A life lived casually is a casualty!

Regret

"If" is the smallest word for regret.

*   *   *

If we would think twice about everything we did we'd probably think twice as much as we do, and we could probably do twice as much as we think, and we'd probably do only half as much as we have done.

*   *   *

Sorrow comes from two sources: regret and compassion.

*   *   *

Afraid to live, afraid to die,
Afraid to love, afraid to cry,
Afraid to fail, so we fail to try.

Resentment

Resentment is the infection that turns a wound into a disease if not treated properly.

Don't let emotional injury damage your soul.
Whether you're burned by bad business, or cut by
cruel comments, or your heart is broken from a poor
relationship, the pain is much the same — and it's
how we handle it that determines how we'll heal.
All our wounds are either malignant or benign,
depending on how we treat them. We'll either get
bitter or better. Don't let your afflictions become
infections! Don't let your canker become a cancer!

Self-control

I have never understood why men curse God in their
time of trouble; that's when they need Him the most.

*   *   *

The only power that conquers sin is the power of
discipline.

*   *   *

Dealing with Anger
In dealing with anger,
It's easier to explode
Than to explore.
But it's a lot easier
To talk it out
Than to rebuild a good rapport.

*   *   *

Many people won't accept the truth because they
don't want to be held accountable, but if they
understand that much it's too late, they are already
accountable.

Anything taken in excess becomes poisonous!

*   *   *

The best thing to do when others are out of line is stay in place.

*   *   *

Either we display composure or we display de-composure.

*   *   *

Having good timing is a lot more important than having a good time!

*   *   *

Condition your mind so that you won't mind conditions.

Work

The two most useless things we can do are worry about things we can't do anything about and worry about things we can do something about.

*   *   *

If the last shall be first and the first shall be last, we'd most certainly better get started!

*   *   *

A man who is not afraid to work has nothing to fear, except maybe, unemployment.

*   *   *

All things work together for good for those who work together for good. (Romans 8:28)

*   *   *

Nothing falls in place; we have to put it there.

*   *   *

Man's greatest occupation is preoccupation. His biggest pastime is trying to figure out how to use it.

*   *   *

If you're having a lot of fun, no work is getting done.

Selfishness

Selfishness is the master of ignorance.

* * *

Selfish listeners listen only to reply, not to comply
or satisfy.

* * *

I believe that Jesus Christ is the only man who ever
walked on this earth who wasn't selfish. He's the only
man who gave everything he had away. Just think
what we'd all have if we would follow his example.

* * *

It's hard to say "I'm sorry" when you're feeling sorry
for yourself.

* * *

The servants are the masters; the selfish are slaves.

The law of supply and demand doesn't mean we can demand our supply.

* * *

Those who center on themselves make a small circle.

* * *

Just think what could be accomplished if we'd stop taking our time and start giving it.

* * *

Selfishness is shallow and shows on the surface, but selflessness has a far deeper purpose that shows through the service.

* * *

A person isn't selfish because he does things for himself. A person is selfish when he does things for himself at someone else's expense.

* * *

He was so at one with himself that he had no room for anyone else.

Greed

It's okay to have possessions as long as they don't possess you.

Greed is an addiction. It's the craving to feed a need after it's already been fed.

*   *   *

Greed is what results when a want becomes a need; when excessiveness becomes a necessity.

*   *   *

I thought the most pitiful man I'd ever met in the world was the man who wanted everything until I met the man who wanted nothing.

*   *   *

It's not getting what you want, but knowing what
    you need
that truly separates ambition from greed.

Pride

An argument is a battle of pride. No matter who wins the war, there is damage to each side.

*   *   *

It's a weak man who's so tough that he can't show his weaknesses.

*   *   *

Sometimes it's better to admit you're wrong than to hurt others proving you're right.

Which of these two men
Hides the most evil inside:
The man too proud to admit he's wrong,
Or the man that forces the other
To swallow his pride?

*   *   *

Pride is moral suicide.

*   *   *

Man can only follow one force.
He can only heed one voice;
Either pride or conscience, never both.
He has to make a choice.

*   *   *

There are countless numbers of men who stuff their
puffed-up attitudes with poisonous pride, but name-
less few who can swallow even the smallest amount
of it to fill their starving souls with the sweet fruits
of humility.

Self-Worth

Men should never be so sure of themselves that they purposely make others doubt themselves. We should be sure to make others sure of themselves.

*   *   *

Nobody is a nobody.

*   *   *

We should never use our convictions
To make others feel convicted,
But to make them feel convinced.

*   *   *

It takes a lot of faith to believe in yourself in a world of nonbelievers. But believe in yourself and others will believe in you also, and then people will begin to believe in themselves.

*   *   *

You can know where you stand and still be lost!

* * *

Our faith is just a dust collector on the shelf until we learn to believe in ourself.

* * *

Sometimes we are so restricted by our securities and insecurities that we cannot reach our potentials. We are like the large elephant who is bound by a frail cord but cannot break free because he believes he is too weak to do so.

* * *

Those who speak for others must not have much to say for themselves.

* * *

Why me? Why not?

* * *

A man only has what he is, nothing else is really his.

* * *

A bad temper will never rest. It is always ready to be manifest.

Identity

Do we get so caught up in pretending to be someone
that we aren't that we forget who we really are, until
we eventually become someone we never wanted to
be? If we can't be ourselves, who are we?

*   *   *

When you're lost, don't speed up!

*   *   *

It's kind of funny how many kinds of things are done
by people who aren't that kind of person.

*   *   *

I don't dislike anyone, but sometimes I dislike what
someone does that reminds me of what I dislike
about myself.

Innocence

No one has ever outgrown innocence
But many have lived and learned
Until it is unknown, in a sense.

*   *   *

Innocence

Innocence is every man's divine inheritance.
Somewhere between ignorance and intelligence we
progress, learn and grow by experience, but we do
so at a certain expense. And though we repent to
repair the dents in our damaged conscience, we can
never remove or erase the evidence that our mind
replaces for lost innocence.

Sin

We can't win a race while running in place.
We can't win a war by fighting no more.
We can't conquer sin while Satan's within.

*   *   *

Bad thoughts can become malignant, like a disease
that spreads and corrodes the mind till it destroys
the thinking processes and the power to reason.

*   *   *

Sometimes the truth hurts, but it only hurts those
who don't live it, and the hurt's not nearly as bad
as the long-lasting injuries of sin.

*   *   *

The only power that conquers sin is the power of
discipline.

*   *   *

Those who covet are those who sacrifice other people's success for their own failure.

*   *   *

I've learned that there are two approaches to both truth and transgression. We can ignore it or explore it.

*   *   *

Does the dirt in our lives pollute the pools of living water that the Savior provided? If the water seems unpleasant it's because we've corrupted the truths and turned them into mud puddles.

*   *   *

Never clip the wings of those who soar!

*   *   *

Solomon and all his wisdom was still deceived by lust and greed. The two oldest vices known to man are still the easiest to heed.

*   *   *

The world is becoming so liberal that suggestion's becoming literal.

*   *   *

Even though the Lord cannot look upon sin,
That doesn't mean we can't pray.
Our Heavenly Father can still hear our prayers
While he is looking away.

* * *

The world has been cooking up iniquity since its creation, and it won't be long until it'll be burned!

* * *

Criminals are an example of how we pay for other people's sins also.

* * *

Think about the sin you're about to commit; imagine the pain it caused the Savior when he atoned for it.

* * *

How much of the forbidden fruit do we partake every day of our lives?

* * *

If everyone's doing it, it's usually wrong,
For it's in great numbers that evil grows strong!

* * *

Sin is the poison of the soul;
Of this every prophet wrote,
And he who procrastinates repentance
Does not take the antidote.

*   *   *

There are three necessary evils:
   1. The temptations of Satan,
   2. The fall of Adam,
   3. The sacrifice of Jesus Christ.
Evil itself is necessary for opposition.

*   *   *

Sin leaves no marks upon our lives
That repentance can't erase,
But the ink stains the soul
When its marks are retraced.

*   *   *

No fish is at home in hot water, and they usually get
burned or boiled before they realize the water keeps
getting hotter!

*   *   *

The effect of sin is always subtle, but it only takes
a little dirt to make a mud puddle.

Dishonesty

One of the most evil forms of deception
Is making someone believe that you believe
that they are something that they are not.

*   *   *

Deceit is just dishonesty in an uglier disguise.

*   *   *

Lies aren't easier to believe than the truth, they're
just faster at getting your attention.

*   *   *

An ounce of pretension, a pound of unsure.

*   *   *

As long as you're dishonest,
It's always the same.
No matter how much you score,
It's a pointless game.

Hypocrisy

It is my desire to see; and to be seen without others
seeing it as being seen of others.

*   *   *

Hypocrisy is using the right to make others think we're right, and they're wrong; while knowing what we're doing is wrong.

*   *   *

A hypocrite is one who sees every rock along life's pathway as a stone for casting at the sinful, and yet never remembers the one man who really has the right to cast them.

*   *   *

Why is it that those who find the truth become humble, or else they become hypocrites?

*   *   *

How many testimonies are torn to bits
Because of the example of hypocrites,
And how many of these examples will one day be
A testimony of their hypocrisy?

*   *   *

I believe it is pharisaical presumption to accept our own solutions as absolutions! There is only one author of truth.

*   *   *

He who has eyes to see, let him see, but not invade other's privacy. And he who has ears to hear, let him hear, that he may learn the truth, rather than hypocrisy.

A hypocrite is a man who quotes himself while speaking about humility.

Lies

What good is a contract? Written promises can be broken just as easy as spoken ones; there's just more red tape to mess up the communication. If our word is no good it won't be any better by writing it down.

*   *   *

A liar has to have a good imagination to come up with so many stories, and a good memory not to repeat them.

*   *   *

Excuses make poor alibis. Their confessions only convict us of lies.

*   *   *

Truth has no boundaries and has no ends
Except where the truth stops and the lie begins.

Procrastination

Procrastination is the riskiest form of gambling.

*   *   *

I wonder how many lives are wasted from confusing procrastination with patience, and how many blessings are postponed from premature anticipation?

Rationalization

I'm amazed at how many Christians believe in the "sale of indulgences" and don't even realize it. They believe they can live certain commandments faithfully and that will pay for the sins they commit.

*   *   *

Rationalization is the ability to lie to yourself about something until you believe it.

*   *   *

Isn't it strange how people can't be forced to do anything, but after just a short period of degeneration, they do it on their own?

*   *   *

You cannot go the extra mile and take short cuts!

Temptation

It's a wise man who can avoid temptation instead of allowing himself to be tempted and then overcome it to prove himself. Proof is the strength of weak men. The best way to prove your strength is to use it to avoid temptation. Remember, we worship Satan when we allow ourselves to be tempted.

In the constant battle between Satan and men
there is also a war that rages within
Between the determination we have to win
and the lack of determination to begin.

*   *   *

We cannot invite sin in and expect the Devil to leave
at our will. We cannot go to the house of Satan and
then throw him out.

*   *   *

"The Devil made me do it"
is the worst excuse
man could ever moan;
the Devil may tempt him
to start out, but
he finishes on his own.

*   *   *

He is always out of control who lets passions pilot
his soul.

*   *   *

Think before you act: a little contemplation can
conquer any temptation.

*   *   *

The difference between Joseph and David was in the
direction they took after the temptation and the
direction they took their contemplation!

Truth

Someone who understands the truth feels no need to argue about it.

*   *   *

We spend so much time asking questions that we never accept the answers to them. There is no reason to ask if we don't want the answer.

*   *   *

Many people won't accept the truth because they don't want to be held accountable. But if they understand that much it is too late, they are already accountable.

*   *   *

Question is the attraction of thought and the attachment to truth.

*   *   *

Those who hunger after truth don't get fed up with learning, but they do have to put up with small meals.

*   *   *

Truth is sometimes raw, and it's always well done, but it's never rare.

*   *   *

The truth hurts the worst for those who use it to hide the truth or to hide from it.

Applied

When we remain true to the truths we have learned, Then much more truth we will have earned.

*   *   *

Sometimes the truth hurts, but it only hurts those who don't live it, and not nearly as badly as the long-lasting injuries of sin.

*   *   *

When you discover the truth it becomes perception, but when you disguise the truth it becomes deception.

*   *   *

Our mission in life is not to seek proof of the truth, but rather to be proof of the truth.

There are too many exceptions to the rules and not enough accepting them!

*   *   *

How the truth fits into our lives depends upon the adjustments, alterations, and arrangements we make. Unfortunately, too many of us try to change the truth to fit our lives instead of changing our lives to fit the truth.

*   *   *

The truth hurts because it hits us where we are the softest.

*   *   *

What good is the truth if you don't know where to put it?

*   *   *

They cannot tell the truth who do not keep it.
They cannot keep the truth who do not tell it.

*   *   *

If the truth seems tough and hard to chew,
Then don't swallow it for a minute or two.
If you can't digest it, what good will it do?

*   *   *

No matter the purpose or how deep you dive, you have to surface for the truth to survive.

Recognized

I have learned that everything
Contains bits and pieces of the truth,
But the distorted sources they are mixed with
Make them appear uncouth.

                *   *   *

As long as we are headed in the right direction,
We all will stumble over the same truths.

                *   *   *

Sometimes when I'm meditating, I discover a truth. But it is not my truth, it is THE truth. Truth does not belong to any one person. Truth is ready for anyone who is ready for it. Truth is eternal.

                *   *   *

I've learned that there are two approaches to both truth and transgression. We can ignore it or explore it.

                *   *   *

The truth is either obvious or oblivious, depending on where you are.

                *   *   *

Truth is often cleverly disguised with circumstance and is not easy to recognize, but if it was, it wouldn't be worth much.

*   *   *

Truth never changes but it does change shape. It is shaped into the form of an individual's perception and understanding. But no matter what form it takes, it is always the same.

*   *   *

All the truth that I have learned teaches the same truth, and the truth I continue to learn confirms it.

*   *   *

How can those who don't look for the truth in everything find it in anything?

*   *   *

It's a lot easier to collect the truth than to recollect it.

*   *   *

The birth of new ideas comes from the conception of truth.

*   *   *

There are those who are "ever learning and never able to come to the knowledge of the truth," and those who are ever learning until they come to the knowledge of the truth. May everyone be learning the knowledge of the truth. (2 Timothy 3:7)

* * *

Too often the meanings and messages are so dressed up with words that the truth gets disguised and unrecognized. Our words don't have to be best-dressed to be expressed!

* * *

Some don't know where the truth is found,
And some know where it's at;
To some the truth is bound,
And they have the answers pat;
Some think the world is round,
And some think the world is flat.

* * *

Behind the lies and disguise,
I can still recognize
The truth within your eyes.

Values

There will be those who will challenge you to do evil by calling you afraid. This is when your true colors will show. Are you yellow, or are you gold?

*   *   *

The only real way to broaden your horizons is by raising your standards.

*   *   *

It's a lot easier to take a cold shower than to get out of hot water!

*   *   *

If everything goes over your head then maybe your head is not in the right place.

*   *   *

In many ways people live their lives like a fairy tale. Too many frogs think they are princes and too many princes think they are frogs.

With what doth thy cup runneth over?

*   *   *

A man with values is very rich because there is nothing more valuable than values.

Honesty

What good is a contract? Written promises can be broken just as easily as spoken ones; there's just more red tape to mess up the communication. If our word is no good it won't be any better by writing it down.

*   *   *

A good man has honesty and always keeps his promises, but a great man has integrity and doesn't have to make promises to help others.

*   *   *

There are very few people who live their life so that they can be themselves no matter who they are with. A person isn't completely honest until he can be himself with everyone.

Priorities

Never allow yourself to become so divided that the portions are too small to work with.

*   *   *

You can tell what possesses a man by his possessions.

* * *

There seems to be a great gulf fixed between what
I like and what I lack.

* * *

Priorities
Which is superior and which is inferior:
Our exterior or our interior?

* * *

We must partake of the milk before the meat,
But eventually we'll starve if we don't eat.

* * *

Sometimes our lives become so crowded,
That nothing seems to fit.
That's why we need priorities,
To clean up and organize it.